PHANTOM JOY

poems by

Cindy Mitchell Appleby

Finishing Line Press
Georgetown, Kentucky

PHANTOM JOY

For Nannie, who taught me that enough is everything.
For Emma and Lauren, who helped lead me to myself.

ACKNOWLEDGMENTS

I want to thank the Great Smokies Writing Program and my classmates for their support and encouragement as I started on my poetry journey. I am forever grateful.

Publisher: Leah Huete de Maines
Editor: Christen Kincaid
Cover Art: Cindy Mitchell Appleby
Author Photo:Heather Hambor of HHphotography
Cover Design: Elizabeth Maines McCleavy

Order online: www.finishinglinepress.com
also available on amazon.com

Author inquiries and mail orders:
Finishing Line Press
PO Box 1626
Georgetown, Kentucky 40324
USA

Contents

Brick Pathway

Over half a century ago my grandfather laid a pathway
to the front door made of bricks
positioned end to end gave it a slight curve
meandering between two skinny pine trees
standing either side no longer there.

well-worn crumbling rectangles
broken edges uneven as ground erodes
patches of moss well established grass
make it hidden but each step
memorized familiar.

Valmore and O'Neil

With post-war optimism and late nights,
   after his shift at the cigarette factory,
      he built their house.

Their house long and narrow, with small rooms and big windows,
   surrounded by pine trees, a large pin oak and a dogwood tree
      that would eventually die.

Their house where I watched baby bluebirds leave their nest,
   in the bedroom where a wall held a plaque with his factory wrench,
      "Laid to rest upon retirement".

Their house where I learned to make cakes and fry chicken,
   where crowded and chaotic washing and drying of dishes
      marked the end of every meal.

Their house where I shelled beans while watching *The Price is Right*
   sitting on the same couch we all rested on when sick,
      and she brought us soup.

Their house where I laid on my mom's childhood bed with library books,
   where I slept, after begging to spend the night again,
      jar full of fireflies on the dresser.

Their house where he drew his last breath,
   and her frail mourning hands clutched a coffee mug
      as she sat in the living room.

It held the rhythms that sustained us,
   was our place of returning,
      a testament to *enough*.

Rose Garden

Crude creation
outside the back door
small square of earth with a
crooked cinder block border
yellow peach red pink
fragrant heirlooms
not bred for perfection
arrangements of
imperfect blooms on the table
her way of saying welcome

Clothesline

In the backyard are rusted silver poles,
     plastic cords sagging between,
remnants of her laundry ritual.
     Homemade basket holding
mountains of clothes,
     faithful patience as she waited
for bright blue skies to welcome the task.
     Steady repetition of her hands reaching down,
pegging each item in a tidy row,
     shirts and sheets dancing in a hopeful breeze,
readying themselves for her return.

Chin Up

In the photograph, her head is tilted back,
chin is slightly raised, eyes gaze upwards.
Perfectly painted lipstick reveals a coy, half smile.
White blouse with short cap sleeves, a handbag under her arm.
Sun pulses through gaps in the trees.

On it she had written in her neat cursive,

> *This is to prove*
> *my chin is still up.*
> *I love you darling.*
>
> *Your wife,*
>
> *Valmore.*

Gardenia

Smell this, she would urge
and press her Joy up to my nose
bright white flower with vivid green leaves
delicate scent a white magic
outside her back door

The Sewing Room

It was our back room escape
where windows looked over camellia bushes and the rose garden.
Where I found thrill in lifting the heavy lid of her cedar chest,
home to stacks of fabric remnants collected over the years.
She taught me how to cut out patterns, thread needles, and pin hems.
On scraps, I practiced sewing straight lines,
rhythmic patterned pulses echoing in my ears.
Here I learned to mend what was broken and create a new
under her watchful eye.

Unexpected

tiny, wallpapered bathroom
hypnotic display of pink and fuchsia flowers
vertical pastel stripes prudently divided
by thin, white wainscoting.
Little girl lingers,
in a room of ritual
the bold color transporting her
to unexpected joy.

Pound Cake

Index card recipe, now faded and brown,
mix butter and sugar
cracked eggs, one by one
sifted flour
alternating milk
don't forget the vanilla.
Scrape the sides
lick beaters and bowl
a cloud of rich batter floats into the Bundt pan.
Golden brown, patterned perfection emerges,
extra thin slices make it go a long way
and she'd say, n*ow isn't that good?*

Sunday Hands

We all sit in the same pew each Sunday. Pa carved out a small, discreet chunk into the back of it so he always knew where to sit. I watch him walk down the aisle and run his hand along the back of the seats to feel for the notch. We slide into the pew and he hands me half a piece of Juicy Fruit gum from the pack he always has in his coat pocket. I pick up an offering envelope and stubby pencil, doodling to pass the time until Nannie finally arrives. I make sure she sits beside me so I can play with her hands. I spin her rings around her delicate fingers, gently pull off her birthstone ring to touch the red ruby that marks my existence. I stroke the back of her hand to feel her soft, papery skin, lightly push down on raised veins to marvel at my power to stop life, ease pressure to watch it suddenly flow again. Until it is time to sing, for her hands to reach out for the hymnal. She urges me up and her fingertips run along each word as we stand there together singing.

Inadequate

Hot summer graveyard day bodies
crowd awkwardly under an insufficient
tent hellish Southern heat forces
the service to be rushed
my feet are frozen by the betrayal
of leaving her here but
finally I follow my brother
who reaches his hand towards her casket
grazes it with fingertips barely audible
he mutters through tears

Estate Sale

We are preparing for an estate sale, although no one would mistake the house for an estate. Her belongings are spread out across every available surface: baskets, blankets and canning jars neatly arranged on rickety folding tables set up where a couch used to be. My job is to determine how much the items of her life are worth by affixing clumsy colored price dots to memories, deciding if blue gloves that once held her hands are worth one dollar or two. She has left no instructions. On the counter in the utility room are the board games my brother and I used to play in the summer. The Candyland box is water-stained and faded, held together by brittle rubber bands. No one will want it, even though all the pieces and cards are still inside. I put it in my pile to take home, unable to put a price on the memory.

Purple Afghan

I didn't want it. Cheap yarn and large holes, varying shades of unexpected purple. I remember her knitting it, sitting beside her on the couch. Her attempts to teach me, needles clumsy in my small hands. We are getting rid of her things, and my mother now offers it to me. I can't reject the gift, the memory of her hands. At home, I toss it across a chair in my bedroom, colors loud against calm earth tones. As the days get colder, I find it calling to me, wanting to lay across my legs, its scratchiness demands I pay attention.

Empty

I walk through the house saying goodbye, sit on the floor in her bedroom and stare at the blank space above where her bed used to be. I fix my gaze on a square of unfaded floral wallpaper where had previously hung a small sampler reading, "To Love and Be Loved is the Greatest Joy on Earth". I take it as a reminder.

The house is mostly empty now, revealing shabby carpets and cracking dull walls. I walk through the house seeking grief, so I can let it go. I sit on the couch in my spot for the last time, try and imagine her sitting across from me in her blue chair. Sitting very still, I wait to feel her comfort wash over me,

but nothing comes.

Flying

My grandmother dreamed
of flying
a bird
soaring above the world.
I dream of driving
a bridge
flood waters
rising up
to consume me.

Phantom Joy

hits like soft morning light finding gossamer strands,
shimmering between leaves of the gardenia bush that is yet to bloom,
only minutes later it disappears

Vacuum

She was vacuuming that morning,
a steady roar pushing across
golden yellow carpet,
repetitive sharp strokes attempting
to distract her from pain,
frantic passing of time,
weary of waiting for me
now two weeks late,
resisting what was outside
of her womb,
a prophecy of my future,
and the beginning of my refusals,
my lack of enthusiasm for a world
of loud distractions,
that attempt to relieve our pain.

Sandcastles

When I was young, my mom sat beside me at the ocean's shore, and we made dribble castles. Our handfuls of wet sand created tall, narrow towers; each drop balanced precariously on the one below it. Delicate structures capable of being destroyed by the waves at a moment's notice.

This summer while walking along the beach, I saw a child sitting in a tide pool, a wall of sand around them made of these clumsy and imperfect towers, decorated with bits of reed and shells. The child was joyous and seemed to have no fear of it all collapsing.

Power

Young girl spins
arms outstretched,
wind pushes and pulls trees,
their rustling leaves clap,
encourage her
invisible power
tendrils of hair
tickle her cheek,
releasing her smile.

Southern Mom

She wrapped our sneakers in Wonder Bread bags
so we could play in the snow, a rare thrill
when silent white covered dull brown.
Anything for a moment of peace
while her children romped around outside,
their sneakers awkwardly covered with evidence
of her frugal devotion.

Sanctuary

I held you both in the center
of my body
where the expansiveness of you
took over.
Vying for more and more
room you stretched
the skin along my abdomen
until it pulled away
from itself
creating white rivers of surrender.
In every direction
you forced yourselves,
desperate to live and grow,
until the time came
and you were each pulled through
a six-inch portal,
sliced with precision.
You both breathed gulps of air,
one of you
more easily than the other,
left behind this skin-shrouded
sanctuary
which now hangs loosely
on my body,
forming the shape
of a smile.

Early Riser

He says the secret to life is to rise early,
but I'd rather stare off into my dreams
where I run down the beach of my childhood.
Stop and roll wildly in the sand,
count the gulls,
watch the waves,
my own sacred liturgy.

Estate Sale II

Instructive notes are everywhere in the house. Slowly dying of cancer gave my mother-in-law time to think about which of her granddaughters would get the pearls, time to let me know the brooch in my hand looks lovely on a dark jacket. A box in the cupboard under the stairs full of silver cutlery includes a note that suggests, *enjoy it all as much as I did.* I wonder if I have.

Floating

I visit the aquarium after my dad's surgery
because I am tired of sitting in plastic blue-green chairs,
and who knows how long it takes to recover?
I walk along the street following directions whispered in my ear,
closing time and everyone is leaving but
I need to see the jellyfish. Surviving
for 500 million years, no bones, blood or brain,
still whole without thinking, only sensing, as they float,
pulsing rhythmically, their transparency shimmering in the dark.

5

The doctor asks me my level of pain, but
what he doesn't know is that my answer is always 5;
too high is to be a bother,
too low, then what's the point of even being there?
I wonder sometimes what 10 would feel like,
think back to years ago when another doctor told me I
was having contractions.
Shouldn't contractions be a 10?
When I was three, I had to get stitches on my head.
I was hysterical, so my dad had to hold me down.
I feel sure if the doctor would have asked me then,
I would have said 10.
Why does my mind not register what my body is feeling?
Is there an effort to avoid more suffering,
if I should tell the truth?
I'd better answer 5.

Suspension

I remember all the playgrounds
blue, green, red, yellow plastic,
standing for hours with mulch in my shoes
bored and restless, wasting time and
accomplishing nothing, except
when you were on the monkey bars and
I stood underneath, watched your
powerful arms propel you
across the mulch sea
aglow with the thrill
of what your body could do,
your power in suspension,
my power in the willingness to stand underneath
waiting to catch you if you should fall.

Surrenders

1
They start here,
with two hearts beating
then blood
fear I had lost them
fear they were boys
stretching, stretching, stretching,
endless preparation,
prints of their feet on my abdomen.

2
Unexpected delivery and
Mother's Day in the NICU,
someone dared to tell us one of them
might not survive,
while the other one
screamed, screamed, screamed,
for her sister.

3
Constant worrying
if they were eating enough
sleepless nights
crying, crying, crying,
accidentally boiling bottles, again,
her tiny hand pulling the neck
of my sagging, milk-stained shirt.

4
Communicating with more than cries,
crawling, laughing, asking for
more, more, more,
I gave them everything I could,
and there was nothing left,
until she pointed at the picture of a cow in the book I held,
smiled and said *moo*.

5
They grew and
chased the ki-tty,
our chairs turned upside down,
because they challenged each other to climb,
higher, higher, higher.
I watched them fearlessly swing
across monkey bars,
not afraid there was no one below
to catch them if they fell.

6
They invented stuffed animal games,
wrote plays with happy endings, always,
singing, singing, singing.
I juggled everything for their joy,
willing surrenders as
I sat and watched them run
strong and free.

7
Fear returned amplified,
tasted of chalk and smelled of sweat,
this awkward adolescence,
searching, searching, searching,
for belonging.
I searched, too.
Only they could choose
who to let in their doors.
I held my breath.

8
What happens next and who
will they become under all of the
pressure, pressure, pressure,
as they climb ladders that
are slowly sinking in sand?

Illumination

Your inner light shimmers,
casting shadows of curved bones on flesh.
Nearby your heart beats faster,
pushes blood through your veins.
The heat of power surges,
lands on shores exposed
where skin tingles and buzzes,
waves of simultaneous sensations erupt.
Words slot into crevices and create options,
hero or villain,
victim or savior.
Are survival or victory the only options,
or can you let your light illuminate,
be a candle to decorate the dark?

Landscape of Me

My forehead rises up like a mountain and
at its base are sunken eyes,
dark and cavernous pools.
My nose is a rock you can crawl onto,
spread out to warm yourself perhaps after swimming
in a river of tears.
My lips are thin and pink
offering a narrow path to walk.
Six moles all different shades of reddish brown
that resemble small stones,
wrinkles around them ripples of presence.
A hollow, curved dip at the base of my throat
smooth and flat,
a pond that collects words
waiting to be spoken.

How to Be my Beloved

I take my body
to lie still in the grass,
turn my eyes up to the sun.
I promise to have and to hold
myself in awe and reverence.
I honor tangles of shadow and light,
seek contentment in the grace of enough.
I commit to rest as my revolution,
in stillness acknowledge life's terror and beauty.
I cherish waves of emotion,
celebrate resilient risings,
my heart and mind wedded
in a ritual of remembering
what it is to be me.

Wishing

Half a century of wishing candles
pull from me what wants to fly
free like dandelion seeds
soft and faithful breath
delivering
trust it can be mine
and always has been
small pockets of paradise
waiting for me

Unveiling

Sitting on the back deck as the sun sets,
he tells me I should write a poem
about leaves. They are falling from the big oak trees,
sounding like rain as they hit the driveway.
He says there is a sadness in their falling,
but potentially a revelation of beauty to be revealed
behind their bare bodies.
What lies behind them after they
fall, what is in the distance?

Rooted

She nurtured a cutting for me
from the gardenia bush outside her back door, and
I planted it outside my bedroom window,
praying I wouldn't kill it.
Thankfully, it thrived, heavy with white blooms in June,
but I moved away.
Since she has gone, my mom fills in the gap,
rooted one for the new house, and it sits
in a pot, waiting to be planted.
I pray it survives.

Wanting

I must have wanted
to know
kept looking to others
to know
kept looking
out the window to
the birds and the changing sky
for inspiration and
answers to the
unknowing
inside me,
blank space
I think needs filling
like arranging a room
with furniture so that
the scene is perfectly inviting,
and I can curl up on the couch
and proclaim
I am finally home.

Cindy Appleby is a writer, life coach and teacher living in Asheville, North Carolina. She has a degree in Psychology from UNC-Asheville and a Masters in Literacy Education from UNC. She spent many years teaching her 5th graders how to craft poems and stories, and finally began her own poetry explorations during the pandemic by taking an online class through the Great Smokies Writing Program.

This is her first publication. You can find her at www.soul-geography. com.

www.ingramcontent.com/pod-product-compliance
Lightning Source LLC
Chambersburg PA
CBHW020221090426
42734CB00008B/1161